May this book
inspire you to Imagine
your own possibilities!

With love + gratitude,
Dianne
7-13

THE IMAGINE PROJECT

STORIES OF COURAGE, HOPE AND LOVE

DIANNE MARONEY
PHOTOGRAPHY BY MARIO MASITTI

Yampa Valley Publishing
PO Box 4696
Parker, Colorado 80134

The Imagine Project: Stories of Courage, Hope and Love

For more information about book purchases, custom editions, special sales, premium and corporate purchases, please contact Special Sales at SpecialSales@TheImagineProject.com

Book Cover and Interior Design by Jef Burnard
Editing by Helga Schier, PhD
Publishing consulting by Judith Briles, The Book Shepherd

ISBN 978-0-9889951-0-9

Library of Congress Number 2013933219

10 9 8 7 6 5 4 3 2 1

First Edition 2013   Printed in Canada

1) Self Help   2) Inspirational   3) Coffee Table

IMAGINE
PROJECT

STORIES OF COURAGE,
HOPE AND LOVE

contents

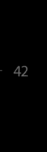

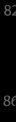

With Gratitude

Creating this book has been the journey of a lifetime. My learning curve was steep, yet the road I traveled was filled with joy, beauty, personal growth, and love.

My deepest gratitude belongs to the beautiful people featured in this book. Your stories, and your willingness to share them with the world will forever inspire me.

Thank you to Mario Masitti. Your generous gift of capturing the soulful essence of the human experience has transformed this book into a tribute to the beauty of the human spirit. Your continuous love of life always makes me smile.

I am indebted to my extended family, friends and even strangers who became friends. Your compassionate ear, your encouragement, and your expertise have been invaluable to me. Know that I will be eternally grateful.

Special thanks go to the keen editorial eyes of Frederic Perrin, Deborah Davis, and particularly Dr. Helga Schier. You are amazing; I couldn't have done this without you.

Thank you to Mario Masitti, Rick Overby, Mandy Lillard Mead, and most of all, Jef Burnard for your beautiful vision in graphic design. Jef, your patience, generosity and creative insight made this book what it is today.

Thank you to Judith Briles, Ken Atchity, Erin Zimmer and Frederic Perrin for guiding me through the process of publishing this book.

My most sincere appreciation goes to my incredible husband, Jimmy, and my three beautiful children, Frank, Michael, and Mackenzie. Your endless patience, tolerance, and support encouraged me to follow my passion. I hope you, too, will always embrace your passion and follow your dreams.

This book has been made possible by the generous financial support of all contributors to our Kickstarter campaign, particularly the following individuals:

The Jonas Family
Paulette Stobaugh Jones
Lloyd Lewis, CEO, arc Thrift Stores
Linda McFall and Patricia Eichelmann
Janet Pasque
Jin Robertson
The Van Tine Family
Stacia Schmalzer
The Zahorik Family

Thank you! Thank you! Thank you!

This book asks you to imagine; to enter a reality other than your own. But it is not a fantasy world I am asking you to explore, and not a better world in the distant future. I am asking you to imagine the very real and present lives of other people; ordinary people, people who surround us every day and everywhere—your neighbors, teachers, co-workers, the clerk at the grocery store, the stranger you pass by on the street, or even the homeless. They are ordinary people, and their lives may seem simple and unremarkable, but if we look and listen closely, we discover tales of love and strength, hope and courage, perseverance and grace.

The journey of *The Imagine Project* began with the birth of my beautiful daughter, Mackenzie. After working at the bedside of tiny preemies for over 13 years, I gave birth to my own very tiny preemie. Until Mackenzie was born, I had always thought I knew what it was like for parents in the Neonatal Intensive Care Unit. Not so. I was immediately humbled. I had to realize that it's impossible to know what it's like to see, feel, and know the experience of someone else, unless we walk in their shoes. Mackenzie's struggles were hard and seemed endless. She was so sick for many years, and many times I felt the despair other parents of preemies must have felt before me. And so I decided it was time to find a way to make health care providers understand the plight of preemies and their parents.

I began speaking at medical conferences around the country, offering my personal story to health care providers. I hoped that my story of a NICU-nurse-turned-mother-of-a-preemie would provide insight into the care preemies and their parent's needs. My speeches began with current information and important medical research, and ended with stories. The stories all began with the word *Imagine*, allowing parents to invite family and friends to empathize and understand their trauma. Writing their *Imagines* brought comfort and awareness to parents, a personal healing of sorts because it gave a voice to their plight, and a deeper understanding of what they had been through. *Imagine*…giving birth to a baby who fits into your hand and may not live for more than a day. *Imagine*…being at home with your baby and finally being able to hold her on your chest for hours.

At every conference, my audience—nurses, doctors, and administrators—would listen in rapt silence as I read these stories. I saw tears and smiles, I heard sobs and laughter, and I witnessed the power of the *Imagines* as they connected human experiences to the invasive tubes and needles and incubators of the NICU. And it is this humanity that nurses, doctors, and administrators took back to their jobs, hopefully influencing their interactions with preemies and parents in a positive, caring, and compassionate way.

Adversity and challenge, hardship and heartache are part of the human experience. With courage, determination, compassion, and love, we can help each other to reach beyond our own comfort zones. And so I took the idea of the *Imagine* stories and widened my search, asking people other than parents of premature babies to write down their stories as well.

Their stories became this book.

It is my hope and my dream that reading this book will encourage you to reflect upon your own stories. What made you who you are? What has shaped your needs, your fears, your beliefs, your hopes, and your pride? While you may wish not to have had some of the more unpleasant, sad, hard, scary, or downright dangerous experiences in your life, you *can* appreciate how these experiences have shaped you. You are who you are because of the life you've lived. And it is up to you how you live with who you've become. Our present and our future are informed by our past. If you embrace your life—the good and the bad and the ugly—if you know and accept who you are and where you came from, you *can* create a brighter future.

Each and every one of the individuals in this book holds a special place in my heart. They have touched me in profound ways, and what they have given me will continue to influence my life. The beauty of their faces, the love and courage of their hearts, and the humility of their souls will forever move me.

I hope that at least one of the incredible people in this book will inspire you, too.

With love and hope, Diane

Imagine a world where kindness and compassion are not the exception, but the norm.

JASON LANDERS

Jason's tall, handsome stature makes it hard to believe he could have ever been bullied. His kind, gentle nature, along with his wisdom and intelligence are immediately apparent. As one sits and talks with Jason, he is open to sharing his struggles in life. Jason was bullied from first grade through high school. After going into the military to get away from life at school, he was bullied again by his platoon. Jason has often lived in a world of hate and judgment. Yet he speaks of hope and a desire to help change the many problems he's witnessed and experienced in life. Through his research and writing in his classes, he finds a greater understanding of what's happened to him. Jason is working toward becoming a lawyer and hopes to share his journey with others so change will happen, protecting other vulnerable children, men and women from bullying in our world.

alive

IMAGINE…

    finding out your best friend slept with your girlfriend.

IMAGINE…

    refusing to trust your family, let alone your friends with the experiences that haunt you.

IMAGINE…

    spite, anger and revenge plaguing your heart; the result: terrible finances, 17 jobs, 14 residences, and four serious girlfriends in the six years following your discharge.

IMAGINE…

    knowing you will die if you don't get help.

JASON LANDERS

IMAGINE...

going to therapy weekly, taking medication daily.

IMAGINE...

crying for the first time in years and feeling alive.

IMAGINE...

going back to school and maintaining a 4.0.

IMAGINE...

people, knowing your pain, accepting you for who you are.

IMAGINE...

beginning to reconcile with your family and being proud of who you are.

IMAGINE...

forgiveness becoming your most powerful weapon in your struggle to survive.

DR. JIN KYU ROBERTSON

It seemed fitting to photograph Jin in front of the Walt Disney Concert Hall. Hers is the rags-to-riches story that reminds you of a Disney fairytale. Jin was born in Korea, where gender equality was not yet a reality, and girls were considered useless. She grew up desperately poor, felt unwanted and hated her life. Today, she is an American citizen, affluent, and highly educated with a PhD from Harvard.

Jin travels around the world speaking about how she transformed her life. Her dreams of a better life allowed her to overcome her fears and overwhelming challenges. Whenever she felt distraught, she'd let her imagination take over, dreaming of a future with possibilities—even for women. "Visualize what you want in life and make it happen." Jin inspires people all over the world to dream, and to make dreams become real one step at a time. "Begin with what you have and take action. Even if the step is small, take it."

equality

IMAGINE...

being born a girl in a small fishing village in Korea.

IMAGINE...

your angry grandmother leaving you in a cold dark corner of a room because, in your society, a baby girl is deemed worthless.

IMAGINE...

watching waves of refugees flood into your village the day the Korean War began.

IMAGINE...

knowing your mother had to risk her life selling goods on the black market so your family could eat.

IMAGINE...

your sister being married by the town's matchmaker, not by choice, destined to lead a poor, unhappy life.

IMAGINE...

people telling you the same fate awaits you because you are a stupid female child and will amount to nothing.

IMAGINE...

a teacher reading your palm and telling you that someday you will be something special.

IMAGINE...

attempting to commit suicide because your dreams of higher education are crushed and a life as a housemaid awaits you.

IMAGINE...

reading about a job as a housemaid in faraway America.

IMAGINE...

landing in New York City with only $100 to your name and no way to return to your country of birth.

IMAGINE...

the joy of becoming a US Citizen.

IMAGINE...

joining the US Army.

IMAGINE...

sending your seven-month-old baby girl to Korea to escape the abuse of your 7th degree black belt husband.

IMAGINE...

telling your baby girl she can be all she wants to be.

IMAGINE...

being the only Korean woman in your platoon.

IMAGINE...

commanding over 200 male soldiers.

DR. JIN KYU ROBERTSON

IMAGINE...

being the first woman to serve as a Foreign Area Officer for the US Army, a prominent title, but a male-oriented society.

IMAGINE...

achieving the highest score ever on your exams, your daughter matching your score twenty years later.

IMAGINE...

retiring from the military and graduating from Harvard with a PhD at age 57.

IMAGINE...

a documentary being made about you, and returning to your village in Korea as a national hero.

IMAGINE...

selling over a half million copies of your memoir and inspiring people from around the world to follow their dreams.

IMAGINE...

knowing that girls can be all they can be.

LAURA SIERRA

Laura received the devastating news that she had Stage IV breast cancer at the same time she was facing unemployment as a newly divorced mother of two young children.

Reaching deep inside, she found the strength to fight an overwhelming sense of defeat and overcome her fears of an uncertain future. She set her priorities straight, putting her two children and her own health first, got a job as a teacher, and moved into a new, more affordable neighborhood. Getting up every day to nurture her children and teach classrooms full of students provided a sense of purpose and order that helped her through nauseating and painful treatments.

Laura refuses to take no for an answer. She continues to receive chemotherapy every three weeks, and her most recent scans showed no evidence of disease. A good dose of humor allows her to appreciate the simplicity of her chemo "haircut" and to laugh with those around her when her fake eyelashes accidentally attach to her sweaters. Laura appreciates each moment with her growing, insightful children, and tries to touch lives every day through her work as a high school teacher.

hope

IMAGINE...

being 38, a single mother of a 5-year-old son and a 3-year-old daughter, and hearing your doctor's voice say the words, "You have terminal breast cancer."

IMAGINE...

calling your parents, siblings and friends to tell them you will die.

IMAGINE...

holding your breath as you hear your father sobbing, a thousand miles away, and knowing that words cannot comfort him.

IMAGINE...

driving to a counseling session with your children, wondering if therapy can prepare them for the day they will have to bury their mother.

IMAGINE...

realizing it can't.

IMAGINE...

waking up in the middle of the night, finding your daughter in her room, arms outstretched, tears running down her cheeks, still dreaming, and calling out, "Mommy, Mommy, don't leave me!"

IMAGINE...

wondering if anyone hears your pleas for your children to live happy, healthy lives, even if it means losing your own to cancer.

IMAGINE...

wondering if there is a God, if He has a plan for you, and why He chose you to have cancer.

IMAGINE...

a warm summer day at the pool with your children, watching tears well up in your son's eyes as other children point and laugh as they talk about you, his mother.

IMAGINE...

making a conscious decision to stop praying for more time, and to start hoping for the strength and wisdom to make the most of the time you have left.

IMAGINE...

your disbelief as you hear your doctor's voice say the words, "No evidence of disease."

IMAGINE...

the smiles on your children's faces as you hold them tight and tell them you will live.

IMAGINE...

a world where "cancer" no longer means "death".

STACY BARE

Tall and strong, trustworthy and compassionate, Stacy exudes the confidence of a natural leader. Leading men in battle had been a childhood dream, yet it has played out a bit differently than he expected. After his trials in the war and battling emotional wounds after discharge, Stacy has found another way to lead men and women. He started *Vet Expeditions*, a nonprofit organization to help others like himself overcome the emotional injuries incurred by their experiences in the military. Stacy challenges vets to conquer not only mountains, but also their fears, helping them find a lost belief in themselves, as well as a new beginning along the way.

Stacy is currently in charge of all outdoor programs for the *Sierra Club*. He lives in Utah and feels great satisfaction that his job offers the opportunity to help others peace

IMAGINE...

being 11 years old and knowing you want to lead men into combat.

IMAGINE...

getting an ROTC scholarship and feeling like you got picked first in the NFL draft.

IMAGINE...

a barracks room full of 18 other men.

IMAGINE...

knowing that statistically, three of them will not come back, but you don't get to know who—not yet.

IMAGINE...

going to war in Iraq.

IMAGINE...

war.

IMAGINE...

coming home from war and no one even knows there is a war, much less where that war is on a map.

IMAGINE...

people afraid of you because you went to war.

IMAGINE...

the shallow appreciation of a nation you went to serve and the stinging discrimination because you did.

IMAGINE...

the depression, the suicidal thoughts, losing friends, their lack of understanding, your inability to adjust, the fits of rage, and the isolation of returning home from war.

IMAGINE...

feeling granite, earth, solidarity in your hands as you go vertical on a rock face for the first time since coming home from war.

IMAGINE...

being on the side of a mountain, and the sense of utility…the sense of self…the sense of purpose coming back to you.

IMAGINE...

on the rock, no one cares whether you went to war or not.

IMAGINE...

bringing this experience to thousands of veterans around the world.

IMAGINE...

bringing non-veterans up on the rock with veterans.

IMAGINE...

a world where non-veterans listen to veterans and take on the burden of reintegration, treating them like normal people, giving them a chance.

IMAGINE...

knowing we are all the same. Don't imagine, just know it.

IMAGINE...

peace.

MOLLY LONG

Molly's life began harshly. Her father left before she was born and passed away before she ever met him. Her mother was an addict for as long as Molly can remember, but has been clean and sober for two years now. Molly grew up poor, she went to bed hungry many times, and her mother often left Molly alone with her younger sister and brother. Before most kids had learned to read, Molly had become the caretaker of her home, supporting her mother, sister and brother. But in a world where surviving seemed to be her only option, Molly began to thrive.

At age 17, Molly all but emancipated herself from her mother's care. Shortly after, she became her younger brother's partial-guardian. She has worked to put herself through college while studying for a double major and is now en route to becoming a nurse-midwife. She travels to the far ends of the world as a volunteer, finding solace in giving to the ill and underprivileged. Molly's beauty, both inside and out, matches blessings

IMAGINE...

being born to a woman who is battered and bruised.

IMAGINE...

trying to understand why your father flees and your mother struggles.

IMAGINE...

somehow your mother endures and finds the strength to tenderly care for you.

IMAGINE...

living beyond the pains of hunger and the filth of maggots and cockroaches...finding ways to cook and clean before you're tall enough to look into the sink.

IMAGINE...

losing sight of reasons to live when those who love and care for you disappear and the light fades.

IMAGINE...

your grandmother, the only woman left in your life you have faith in, dying, your heart falling so far that when it hits the ground you cannot feel it.

IMAGINE...

a little voice inside you screaming, but you barely release a sob.

IMAGINE...

feeling alone and heartbroken before you understand what heartbreak is.

IMAGINE...

a life touched by grace and being given a second chance to live.

IMAGINE...

filling your lungs with gasping breaths of air as your whole body fills with purpose.

IMAGINE...

not knowing where your next meal is coming from or where life is taking you, but feeling warmth from within.

IMAGINE...

love conquering the sadness, constantly encouraging you to keep living.

IMAGINE...

looking back and feeling grateful for all the heartache and every blessing.

IMAGINE...

not wanting to imagine any other life...knowing you are here today because of yesterday, and here today for your life tomorrow, but most importantly, knowing you are here today to live, love, and be free.

JAY STAHLMAN

Watching Jay interact with his brothers is humbling. He embraces them for who they are and feels no shame or embarrassment. In fact, Jay didn't think twice about picking the word 'Pride' to represent his story. Jay is proud of his family. He believes it's always important to remember where you came from and respect what made you the person you are. To him, this is self-confidence. "If you take pride in your family, your actions, and yourself, you'll be content with life no matter the outcome."

Jay recently graduated with a Bachelor of Science degree in Economics from Whitworth University in Spokane, WA. He is attending graduate school to get his Master's in Business Administration. He plans to find a job in International Business Management and dreams of becoming the CEO of a Fortune 500 company.

pride

IMAGINE...

being three years old and your excitement at hearing the news that a new little brother is on the way.

IMAGINE...

doubling that excitement when you find out it will be twins.

IMAGINE...

the confusion as you listen to doctors try to explain the meaning of "premature" and "cerebral palsy".

IMAGINE...

wheelchairs, computers, therapists.

IMAGINE...

oxygen, feeding tubes, nursing aides.

IMAGINE...

your brothers enduring 23 surgeries combined in the first 10 years of their lives.

IMAGINE...

the survivor's guilt you feel as you grow up walking, running, and playing, while your little brothers spend more time in

It's hard to fathom that anyone could live the life Randle has lived. Drawing on his firsthand experience, Randle teaches us that the homeless are people with a history of hard knocks, mental illness, and difficult choices.

Randle is a well-educated professional with a Master's degree, who lost it all to his own set of hard knocks and bad choices. Today, he gets help in coping with his cruel life experiences, and lives a full life that he embraces. He cares deeply about other people, and puts his experience and education to use running a shelter for the homeless. On behalf of the homeless, he writes, speaks, and works with numerous

RANDLE LOEB

grace

IMAGINE...

your mother being only a few months pregnant with you, when she jumps out of a moving car with the intent to end her life—and yours.

IMAGINE...

always keeping the covers over your head to block out the goblins and spirits that haunt the nightmares of your childhood.

IMAGINE...

no one wanting to be your friend because you can't sit still, you stutter, you can't memorize anything, and you are often unkempt.

IMAGINE...

people saying you are lazy, some thinking you are an idiot, your mother not caring and nobody realizing something is wrong, that you are bipolar and could be saved.

IMAGINE...

being 14 years old and your teacher molests you.

IMAGINE...

your mother knows and does nothing about it. Instead she crawls into bed with you and molests you, too.

IMAGINE...

a marriage years later…then three children you adore, protect, care for…teaching them about literature and songs…taking great pride in their studies, but struggling to love them from your damaged heart.

IMAGINE...

a nasty divorce and separation from your family for years.

IMAGINE...

finally being diagnosed with bipolar disorder at age 44…finding help…getting an education…building a new life.

IMAGINE...

life going well, then a phone call informing you that your daughter has been in a car accident and may not live…staying by her side in a state of terror…feeling responsible for her near death and the deaths of her boyfriend and the baby in her womb.

IMAGINE...

throwing away your medication in anger, neglecting your health, losing your income, your home, everything as your daughter, consumed by her own anger, disowns you.

IMAGINE...

sleeping in a stranger's garage, headlights beaming in your eyes and the wheels of a car coming close to crushing your skull… the shame and humiliation as you drag your dirty bag to another place of momentary protection.

IMAGINE...

trying to sleep and the cops come and you don't know if they will kick the shit out of you, give you a ticket, or harass you until you leave.

IMAGINE...

the hunger, the cold, the fear as you eat out of dumpsters and live on the street.

RANDLE LOEB

getting help, medication, direction…finding a voice…serving on committees that help the homeless…newspaper editing and writing…pursuing your vision that one day society will realize that the homeless are people with a history, too.

IMAGINE…

hoping for reconciliation with your children…hoping for relationships with your grandchildren…hoping one day they will understand.

IMAGINE…

finding grace in every day of your life, no matter what.

CHIP RICHARDS

Chip is a uniquely talented man. He has a wonderful way of making you feel comfortable and relaxed. It's as if he knows and acknowledges your innermost thoughts, and allows you to accept and feel accepted for them, no matter how deep your wounds or worries might be. He touches your soul, finds that candle within, and lights it. Chip breathes and exudes a deep sense of grace and respect.

Chip coaches throughout the world, mentoring individuals in achieving their dreams, advising companies on empowering and unifying employees, and facilitating groups of individuals seeking personal fulfillment. He also writes screenplays and is working on a series of books. An American, Chip lives with his wife and son in Australia, where his coaching career began.

growth

Chris Richardson

IMAGINE...

being the youngest of three boys, hearing stories of ski trips north, but being too young to join.

IMAGINE...

moving to the mountains of Colorado in the winter at age nine…feeling snow plant a seed of destiny inside you on the first day.

IMAGINE...

nurturing that seed into the vision of an Olympic dream in Freestyle Skiing.

IMAGINE...

learning, growing, stretching, becoming…countless early mornings, frozen windscreens, road trips, friendships…
a life emerging from this seed.

IMAGINE...

flying through the air, claiming a number one national ranking…step by step getting closer to your dream.

IMAGINE...

landing one day, just like so many other days—this time with piercing pain.

IMAGINE...

disappointment in your coach's eyes, tears in your father's, as the doctor cradles your knee.

IMAGINE...

reconstructive surgery, first one knee and then the other.

IMAGINE...

angst and frustration, fear of not knowing what rises from the soil of a broken dream.

IMAGINE...

learning to walk again, building strength in new ways, pushing through pain.

IMAGINE...

accepting an invitation to coach for a day…and strangely the pain begins to fall away.

IMAGINE...

accepting an invitation to coach for a season…in Australia of all places.

IMAGINE...

meeting your soul mate in a tiny mountain village on the other side of the world.

IMAGINE...

one season turns into many as the head coach of an Olympic team…a seed of dreams comes to fruition in unexpected ways.

IMAGINE...

waking to a deep passion for the infinite possibilities of human potential.

IMAGINE...

following that passion as a coach not only in sports, but also in film, music and business.

IMAGINE...

learning from CEOs, Native Elders, children and the natural world.

IMAGINE...

looking back on the path and seeing golden lessons each step of the way.

IMAGINE...

writing and speaking these lessons as stories, and guiding others to speak theirs.

IMAGINE...

filming and sharing them with people all around the world.

IMAGINE...

planting one seed and growing a garden so different from what you thought it would be, discovering more colorful dreams every step of the way.

The death of a child is a parent's greatest fear and life's ultimate sacrifice. Sharletta will never forget the death of her son, yet her ability to forgive the three teenagers who took his life is a lesson for us all. Through her faith, she has found a way to look past the loss of her son and see the boys who killed him as just children with troubled lives of their own. In time, Sharletta began to feel empathy. On behalf of the juveniles, and many others like them, she offered her testimony before the Supreme Court, asking to create reformative rather than punitive prison sentences for juveniles convicted of severe crimes.

SHARLETTA EVANS

Sharletta's healing process has taken years, and she still misses her son everyday, but she channels her pain into a nonprofit program that helps keep at-risk kids off

forgiveness

Shantetta

IMAGINE...

moving to another state, away from everything you know and love at the age of seven.

IMAGINE...

being the youngest of 12 children.

IMAGINE...

meeting a spiritual leader at the age of nine, not realizing that he would be your lifelong pastor.

IMAGINE...

losing your faith, making poor choices, living life as you choose.

IMAGINE...

being blessed with a beautiful son.

IMAGINE...

lying in a hospital bed, pregnant with your second child, septic, doctors predicting your death.

IMAGINE...

doctors predicting that your son has received medical interventions during the emergency C-section that will hinder his mobility and that he will likely not be able to live the normal life of a child.

IMAGINE...

turning back to God, vowing that if you live you will come back to Him, and raise your boys in church, teach them the power of God's love and do anything and everything he asks.

IMAGINE...

God answering those prayers.

IMAGINE...

fulfilling every vow you made to God.

IMAGINE...

preparing for Christmas with your children, answering the phone and hearing your niece tell you about a drive-by shooting the night before, asking you to come and get her out of harm's way.

IMAGINE...

rushing to your niece's rescue, then gunshots erupting again, but this time it's your children that are in harm's way.

IMAGINE...

panic as you learn that your three-year-old has been shot.

IMAGINE...

thinking your work is done with the words "I forgive," only to find that these words are just the beginning.

IMAGINE...

realizing what you thought was justice, was in fact injustice.

IMAGINE...

advocating for your child's murderers before the U. S. Supreme Court.

IMAGINE...

the man who took your child's life asking that you love him like a mother.

IMAGINE...

meeting the main shooter who is now a man, and embracing him as if he was your own son.

IMAGINE...

forgiveness.

KAYOKO MITSUMATSU

Kayoko was born in Japan, and moved to the US in 1992. She spent many years living abroad in Australia, Brazil, and the United Kingdom. She is a documentary filmmaker by profession, but her love and passion is yoga. After meeting Nobel Peace Prize recipient Dr. Muhammad Yunus and learning of his work in the micro financing revolution, she decided to use his ideas for a program that would help families in India. Realizing that for the cost of one yoga class anyone can change a life, Kayoko founded a nonprofit organization called *Yoga Gives Back*. With a donation of only $25, an impoverished woman in India can start a business, and a disadvantaged child can go to school. Her passionate documentary film work tells the world about these lives unseen, touching many, many lives every day.

justice

IMAGINE...

growing up in a country during an economic miracle—no wars, but Olympics, World Expos, color TV and bullet trains.

IMAGINE...

in that same country, men earning an income while women take care of the home, children, parents and in-laws, without much appreciation or recognition for their dedication and hard work.

IMAGINE...

being 17 years old and spending one year as an exchange student in Australia, finding a lifestyle where gender does not matter.

IMAGINE...

one year later moving to Brazil with your family, and witnessing extreme poverty, discrimination and inequality.

IMAGINE...

your deeply seeded sense of social justice growing steadily, but not knowing how to give it a voice as you can't even speak the language.

IMAGINE...

becoming a documentary filmmaker years later, telling the stories of people whose voices are often ignored.

IMAGINE...

practicing yoga to keep your body and mind healthy and strong.

IMAGINE...

realizing that for $25—the cost of a single yoga class—you can help an impoverished woman take charge of her life, start a business and end the vicious cycle of poverty.

IMAGINE...

women being able to give their children a better life and an education.

IMAGINE...

knowing deep down that first you live life to experience and learn, and then you live life to serve others and give back.

IMAGINE...

filming the women and children whose lives have improved because someone has given a single yoga class.

IMAGINE...

making the world a better place—one yoga class at a time.

KAYOKO MITSUMATSU

MACKENZIE MARONEY

Mackenzie has a sign on her bedroom door that reads, "Smile, it confuses people."

And she lights up every room with her smile. Mackenzie was born prematurely at one

and a half pounds, a weight that usually spells disaster. Yet from day one, she bravely

fought for what seemed to be her destiny: thriving against all odds. Her outward

beauty matches the depth of her soul, with her eyes revealing her determination,

courage and strength. Knowing her survival is nothing short of a miracle, she embraces

each day, relishes time with family and friends, and never hesitates to laugh hysterically

at the silly side of life.

Mackenzie is studying photography at Watkins College of Art and Design in Nashville.

Using her keen eye and deep appreciation for life, she captures the world around her

through a camera lens, and plans to share her unique vision with the world someday.

strength

Mackenzie Maroney

IMAGINE...

holding your dad's ring in your hand, knowing that when you were born, it could fit around your leg.

IMAGINE...

living the first 3 months of your life in an incubator, your parents can touch you for minutes each day, holding you only when the nurses give them permission.

IMAGINE...

being told you were never supposed to walk.

IMAGINE...

having two big brothers, your heroes, who cried for you, played with you, and pushed you everyday to live a normal life.

IMAGINE...

walking through life a step behind, never knowing if you'll ever catch up.

IMAGINE...

having the love and support of a family of aunts, uncles, grandparents, cousins, second cousins...all pushing you to be the best you can be and NEVER giving up on you.

IMAGINE...

fighting for 17 years to live the best life you can and looking back proudly, knowing you have.

IMAGINE...

you are your father's daughter...daughter of the man who, in those first critical years of your life, believed in you, and always will.

IMAGINE...

loving your mom so much it hurts, for she gave you life, and would give hers for you in an instant.

IMAGINE...

appreciating life with your every breath, for you almost didn't have a life to live.

IMAGINE...

being born weighing only one pound, twelve ounces.

Daniel is a Native American scholar and environmental activist. He is a Yuchi member

of the Muscogee Nation and is currently the acting Dean of the School of Natural

and Social Sciences at Haskell Indian Nations University. He teaches about the

history of Native Americans and the challenges we face in our environment today.

On the phone, in person, and even in an email, Daniel's demeanor is one of grace

and kindness. He sees the world as a joyous place, and recognizes that each moment

lived is a precious gift. His smile and warm embrace speak to the beauty we can

see every day when we stop, observe, and take in the glory of our lives.

DANIEL WILDCAT

beauty

IMAGINE...

watching people with little material wealth sharing what they have with strangers in need—expressions of generosity with no expectations of anything in return.

IMAGINE...

sleeping with your windows open so you can hear owls and coyotes at night, and crows in the morning.

IMAGINE...

living with an artist who expresses her creativity in everything she does; who makes your house a home, a place where just sitting gives you pleasure and makes you feel thankful.

IMAGINE...

watching your wife care for her aging parents and an older sister in your home, not because she could not do otherwise, but because she wants to.

IMAGINE...

opening your tobacco pouch and taking a deep whiff as a feeling comes over you—and memories, too, of your grandfather, for you're filling your pipe with his tobacco now.

IMAGINE...

it is almost midnight, you are tired but need to write because your chapter is long overdue, you open the library door and listen to the wind rustling leaves in the trees and across the yard on a warm October night.

IMAGINE...

it is fall, a late afternoon, and the sunlight fills the room with an amber glow that fills you with gratitude because you are there to see it.

IMAGINE...

standing on a hill in the center of the Konza tallgrass prairie and all you see is an undulating landscape of hills and horizon.

IMAGINE...

an elderly couple walking down the street holding hands and talking.

IMAGINE...

your mother telling you it doesn't matter if you have the best new clothes or the shiniest shoes, because what matters is who you are on the inside.

IMAGINE...

sitting at a table with friends, eating, drinking, telling stories and laughing without any self-consciousness—no one is thinking about entertaining.

IMAGINE...

walking your dog on a cold winter night, the air is clear, the stars are bright, and underfoot, the snow makes a soft crunching sound.

IMAGINE...

living attentively for the tender mercies that don't make headlines.

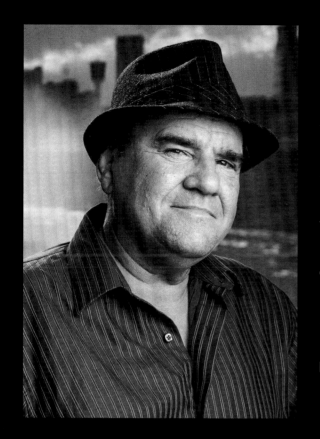

ROBERT G. DEMBIK

Bob faces difficult physical challenges every day of his life. He has to watch every ounce of water he drinks and every speck of salt he puts on his food. He can only walk short distances at a time, because his heart becomes overloaded with fluid easily and needs time to recover. The uncomfortable feeling of fluid retention is with him until his dialysis appointments three times a week. He needs a new kidney or nothing will ever change, but he wonders if he is worthy of getting it—his fourth. Bob wonders if there is someone out there who might need the kidney more than him, yet he knows it is not up to him to decide.

Bob is happy, grateful to be alive, and expects himself to make the best of each moment. He is a fighter; now retired with pride, he looks back on 20 years of diligent work despite his physical challenges. He feels compelled to show the world his beautiful photo of an angel that appears in the mist of Niagara Falls; a sign beckoning him to share his faith in the message that someone or something will always have your back. Bob's will to survive is remarkable; he doesn't just survive, he lives life with a mission to help others believe they can accomplish anything they set out to do.

meaning

Robert A. Dembth

IMAGINE...

starting your freshman year as the worst tennis player of your school and graduating as number one of the varsity team.

IMAGINE...

the courage and fortitude it took to get there.

IMAGINE...

losing your dad the final semester of college and graduating nonetheless, knowing that this is what he would have wanted for you.

IMAGINE...

being 24 years old and learning that you have kidney failure and may not live a long life.

IMAGINE...

the blessing of acceptance as you come to understand how fragile life is.

IMAGINE...

barfing your guts out the first time you are stuck with a 15-gauge needle—the one you will need six times a week just to stay alive.

IMAGINE...

having a long tube attached to your belly with a bag to drag around, having medical treatments every four to six hours to stay alive.

IMAGINE...

realizing that others have a fate far worse than yours, taking comfort in knowing that God has a plan for you.

IMAGINE...

getting back on your horse and having a full life.

IMAGINE...

commuting to work almost an hour each way, working a ten-hour day, performing self-dialysis twice each day, and being on the tennis courts by 7:00 p.m.

IMAGINE...

loving life just because you were able to live it.

IMAGINE...

having your body reject your first and second kidney transplants within a few days, suffering complications, having a 106 degree temperature for two nights, approaching the brink of death.

IMAGINE...

surrendering, accepting whatever plan God might have for you, be it life or death.

IMAGINE...

traveling to Niagara Falls for inspiration, taking a photo of the Falls, and discovering in that photo the "Niagara Falls Angel."

IMAGINE...

finally getting a third transplant—one that lasts ten years.

IMAGINE...

having a cardiac arrest at the airport, having a stranger notice and perform CPR for 25 minutes, saving your life.

IMAGINE...

waking from two days in a medically induced coma, remembering that you saw your parents, who have already passed, standing over you, asking if you would like to come with them.

IMAGINE...

being given a choice to cross over or stay in the physical world.

IMAGINE...

deciding to stick around because you feel you can still make a difference.

IMAGINE...

being immeasurably grateful to the people that inspired you and helped you meet your challenges.

IMAGINE...

thinking of and thanking your donors every day, knowing you will meet them someday, this side or the other.

RACHEL GOBLE

Rachel grew up in what she calls a normal, all-American household. Life was good, health—physical, psychological and emotional—was important, and her parents acknowledged and supported her passions in life. Traveling overseas with her family, she had a chance to see and reach beyond the narrow scope of her safe neighborhood, and her father's lifelong involvement in philanthropic organizations taught her the value of giving.

Living in India while doing research for her Master's degree, she met women and children who live in the horrific world of sex trafficking. Touched by the plight of those sold into sexual slavery, Rachel helped a friend produce a film about this world in Thailand and *The Sold Project* was born, a project providing educational scholarships to children at risk of exploitation. Her dedication and hard work for the project has improved the quality of life for many children, who then have a chance to return to their communities and help prevent sex trafficking at the source.

thrive

IMAGINE...

being born into an affluent family that cares about justice and fairness, exposing you to the world from a young age.

IMAGINE...

being given every opportunity and more as a child, and realizing that this wasn't the norm.

IMAGINE...

developing a passion for children, all children, and wanting them to have the freedom to be children.

IMAGINE...

twenty-seven million people around the world enslaved—most of them children.

IMAGINE...

sitting in a brothel in Bombay, talking with women who tell you, "I'm not like you—I can't just leave here and be free."

IMAGINE...

realizing this didn't have to be their future.

IMAGINE...

realizing you can do something. That everyone can.

IMAGINE...

knowing that changing one life can change the world.

IMAGINE...

a world of prevention, ensuring that every child has the opportunity for education, dreams and freedom.

IMAGINE...

a village once susceptible to sex trafficking now embracing education, opportunity and dreams.

IMAGINE...

a world where every child has the opportunity to thrive.

REV. LEON KELLY

Reverend Kelly can be intimidating. His tall, dominating stature and deep, authoritative voice commands immediate respect. Yet the many children who run up to greet him with a hug everyday when he arrives at his after-school program are evidence that his warmth and genuine caring also command trust. If there is trouble brewing, an argument between the kids or inappropriate behavior towards a teacher, Reverend Kelly immediately deals with each child directly, teaching each and every one of them tools to deal with anger and frustration in accountable and constructive ways.

Revered Kelly has dedicated his life to helping children coming from challenging and troubled homes. He strives to teach them to respect not only others, but themselves, too. He and his wife have four biological children and five foster children. What's more, Reverend Kelly has been a father figure to hundreds of other children who have passed through his anti-gang program.

reverence

Rev Fran Kelly

IMAGINE...
growing up in a house filled with love, guidance, reverence, humility and commitment to faith.

IMAGINE...
your father getting a job that pays $1.25/hour and celebrating with Kool-Aid and "pot of meat" sandwiches.

IMAGINE...
being the firstborn son, the one who is expected to fix what's broken, to know, to lead, to help others.

IMAGINE...
playing football and basketball at a Division I school.

IMAGINE...
falling into the "high life," and liking it.

IMAGINE...
spending money fast, wanting more faster, getting it by selling pot and cocaine.

IMAGINE...
living a double-life as a semi-pro basketball player in a penthouse suite you pay for with drug money, but your family thinks it's all because you're smart and educated and an amazing athlete.

IMAGINE...
carrying three guns for protection, yet finding yourself tied up in a closet waiting to be killed. Being saved because the knife that was meant to kill you sliced the hand of the assassin instead of your neck.

IMAGINE...
the police arresting you, a trial, a three-year prison sentence, and seeing your mother cry when she comes to visit you.

IMAGINE...
following in your father and grandfather's footsteps as you realize that all this was God's way of preparing you for your life's work as a minister.

IMAGINE...
working with gang members at the community center in your old neighborhood, playing ball when one of the kids under your care throws a metal object at a car, hitting the girl in the passenger seat, cracking her jawbone.

IMAGINE...
the utter lack of remorse of those kids.

IMAGINE...
the gang member's younger brother being shot in retaliation, living barely long enough to crawl to his mother's house.

IMAGINE...
an after-school program that connects with at-risk kids early, before the gangs find them.

IMAGINE...
becoming a surrogate father, a mentor, a positive connection to an endless number of kids, hoping to teach them reverence.

starting to understand what it must be like to grow up without a father—and therefore appreciating yours all the more.

IMAGINE...

hoping that someday someone will give enough money to your program so you can train others to do what comes naturally to you—connecting with those who don't know how to connect.

Andy is a natural mom. She is always there to love, listen to, and care for her four grown children and grandchildren. Tenderness, compassion and kindness permeate the room when she is present. She thinks of her firstborn son every day, wondering if their paths have ever crossed, always hoping that one day she will meet the son she gave up for adoption many years ago. Her children know about their older brother, and the idea of meeting him some day makes them smile with anticipation.

Sadness and joy permeate the memories of her first pregnancy. Andy insisted on holding her son and showing him as much love as possible in those three short days she was allowed to be with him in the hospital. This was a closed adoption, but over the course of several years Andy received three letters and a few pictures from his adoptive parents. The search for her son is emotional, time-consuming and costly but Andy eagerly anticipates the day she will be reunited with her son.

ANDREA LOSH

gift

Andy Losh

IMAGINE...

an unexpected pregnancy.

IMAGINE...

being unwed, a teenager and afraid to tell your parents.

IMAGINE...

your choices: Abortion? Raising the child without support? Adoption?

IMAGINE...

knowing this child will be in your heart forever, no matter what you decide.

IMAGINE...

realizing you have a gift for someone who wants, but cannot have a child.

IMAGINE...

having to hide your pregnancy in a town far away from your parents, your siblings and friends.

IMAGINE...

your grief when your beloved grandmother dies while you are away, and the shame when you have to pay your respects in secret so nobody will see your growing belly.

IMAGINE...

your excitement, fear and joy the day you go into labor.

IMAGINE...

the overwhelming love for your baby boy as you hold and love him.

IMAGINE...

giving him a name—Christopher Anthony.

IMAGINE...

your overwhelming sadness as you give him up, and his family's overwhelming joy as they receive him.

IMAGINE...

how hard it is to write this.

IMAGINE...

moving forward in life.

IMAGINE...

marriage, then four more beautiful children—two boys, two girls, each boy with a name that commemorates your firstborn son.

IMAGINE...

remembering him—every birthday, every holiday, every day—and loving him ever more.

ANDREA LOSH

your children thinking of him as their older brother and wanting to meet him one day.

IMAGINE…

your four children growing up, finding jobs, getting married, having children.

IMAGINE…

wondering if he has children, too.

IMAGINE…

hoping you will meet him one day, so you can tell him what a gift he's been to you.

Judith doesn't mince words, she says what she thinks and means what she says.

And if she wants something done, it gets done; if need be, she gets it done herself.

Most of Judith's friends and colleagues don't know the intense ups and downs of her history, but what they do know is that she has a huge heart and loves helping others.

After her business partner and close friend stole all of her personal assets—causing her to lose her home, cars and her health—she told a friend she would never help anyone again. The friend kindly listened and reminded Judith that helping people was ingrained in her soul; she would feel generous again one day.

JUDITH BRILES

Judith doesn't let life get her down. Give her a challenge and she will see the challenge and raise the stakes even higher. Judith is someone you always want in your corner.

passion *pour*

IMAGINE...

learning at a young age that jobs earn money, careers bring passion.

IMAGINE...

being a teen mom, having three kids by the time you are 20, number four on the way when you are 25.

IMAGINE...

losing your baby, going through a divorce, feeling as if your life is over, and discovering that being a Mom was your first true career.

IMAGINE...

being fired from your position as the assistant to a top producing stock broker because you are getting a divorce and your ex-husband was harassing your employer.

IMAGINE...

clients being so incensed they give you money, an airline ticket to San Francisco and a list of job interviews.

IMAGINE...

being one of the first women stockbrokers.

IMAGINE...

losing your children in a horrible divorce battle because the judge believed your husband's lies, discovering that your attorney had been paid by your soon to be ex-husband to undermine you in court.

IMAGINE...

channeling your anger toward your career so you can find a way to get your children back.

IMAGINE...

after your kids are with you for a week's vacation, you tell your ex they are with you for good.

IMAGINE...

the same judge, realizing he'd been wrong, now granting you full custody of your children.

IMAGINE...

a new husband, community and home for your children.

IMAGINE...

becoming so sick with a massive infection that each of your organs begins to shut down and rupture.

IMAGINE...

watching doctors work on you from outside your body, way up above, no longer feeling pain.

IMAGINE...

suddenly re-entering your body and feeling excruciating pain riveting throughout your body.

IMAGINE...

being paralyzed below your waist for months, which helps you find a whole new perspective on life.

IMAGINE...

finding a new career, writing your first book, speaking all over the world and *Good Morning America* calling.

IMAGINE...

challenging academia for your B.A. so you can go back to school to earn your MBA.

IMAGINE...

your business partner and her husband stealing all your assets from a million dollar business.

IMAGINE...

anger, despair and exhaustion awakening the cancer cells in your body.

IMAGINE...

getting back on your feet once again and going back to school to get your DBA.

IMAGINE...

waking late one night to a policeman in your house, saying "I'm sorry, your son is most likely dead...
we will continue searching until daylight..."—he doesn't survive.

IMAGINE...

finding a way to resurrect from your financial hardship and deal with personal disasters, seeding a vision for a new career path and passion.

IMAGINE...

writing 30 more books, acquiring greater expertise, speaking at more engagements, traveling, audiences,
people seeking you out, feeling as if you have found yourself again.

IMAGINE...

so many experiences of loss...finding your way each time.

IMAGINE...

your heart swelling with a passion to support others to write
and publish their own books...once again finding yourself
through helping others .

DOUG CAMPBELL

Doug lives with his second wife, Karen, in a tiny town in the majestic Yampa Valley of Colorado. It seems the beautiful mountain scenery feeds his soul, allowing him to find peace despite losing his son and first wife too soon. There is no calmer, kinder, or gentler man around. Doug's kindness shines through in his open and engaging conversation as he listens with intent and understanding. Meeting him, you know at once he will always have your back.

Doug is retired and spends much of his time being a grandfather to his only grandchild. Many weekends he drives three hours to watch his grandson play football. He takes him hunting, fishing and to just about every outdoor activity there is. His grandson is secure knowing his grandfather loves him and believes in him, while he fills a void in Doug's heart.

resolve

Moose

Douglas Campbell

IMAGINE...

being 17 years old, standing before a judge who is about to fine you for outstanding traffic tickets you cannot pay.

IMAGINE...

the judge telling you that if you join the military, all charges will be dropped.

IMAGINE...

coming home after serving four years on two ships in the Vietnam War, and marrying the most beautiful petite Irish girl with a smile, a twinkle in her eye, and a laugh you could pick out of a crowd.

IMAGINE...

your wife being three months pregnant, but you have no job and no health insurance.

IMAGINE...

finding a job and a career as a locomotive engineer.

IMAGINE...

having two beautiful children with the love of your life, a boy and a girl.

IMAGINE...

coming home at 3:00 in the morning after a long night on the trains, walking into your son's bedroom and finding him dead.

IMAGINE...

waking your wife to tell her.

IMAGINE...

knowing your only son killed himself at age 16.

IMAGINE...

asking yourself why, anguished that you could not prevent it, carrying him in your heart, forever missing him.

IMAGINE...

watching your daughter struggle through pregnancy after pregnancy, losing them all.

IMAGINE...

the joy when she finally delivers a baby boy who is perfect in every way.

IMAGINE...

your wife suffering from emphysema.

IMAGINE...

moving to a small Colorado town so you can take a job that gives you time to care for her.

IMAGINE...

watching her struggle for four long and painful years.

IMAGINE...

calling 911 when the struggle is finally over.

IMAGINE...

watching your mother pass away just days later.

IMAGINE...

staying strong for your daughter and your grandson.

IMAGINE...

looking back on your life, grateful for the good times, grateful even for the bad because that's how you became a more positive, caring person.

IMAGINE...

life as a promise of joy and love.

FRANK & ELSIE POMPONIO

When we think of family, we hope and dream of a family exactly like the Pomponios.

Frank and Elsie radiate love, commitment, faith, inclusion, acceptance, strength, grace, and joy. Watching them interact with their children, grandchildren, and great-grandchildren pulls on heartstrings, creating appreciation, awe, and perhaps even the longing to be born a Pomponio.

Married for 53 years, Frank and Elsie have faced many challenges with their family, but the challenges never seem to get the best of them. When their first grandchild was born with severe disabilities, they believed he was brought to them to shower him with love. To this day, they remain committed to each other, their immediate family, friends who feel like family, and even strangers who need some time in a loving home. Frank is an avid fisherman, hunter, and outdoorsman; so open-minded and compassionate that he is everyone's best friend. Elsie's petite arms are always open, offering love and reassurance through the strength of her hugs. She has won hundreds of tennis matches, and climbed many mountains. Both in their early 80s, Frank and Elsie continue to bike challenging roads across the country, spend time with lifelong friends, and inspire those around them with their health and optimistic outlook on life. Sunday dinners filled with pasta and vivacious fun bring memories to all who are fortunate enough to stop by.

love *Frankie Elsie*

IMAGINE...

coming home from two years in the army during the Korean War at age 25, ready for the easy life—no worries, no pressure, and no thoughts about the future.

IMAGINE...

seeing a girl one day as she's looking over a fence on her tippy toes, and thinking she was somethin'.

IMAGINE...

dreaming that night; dreaming that you are talking to your best friend about a plane crash.

IMAGINE...

waking up the next morning to find out your best friend died in a plane crash that very night.

IMAGINE...

meeting the girl of your dreams at his funeral, the girl on tippy toes.

IMAGINE...

realizing she was your best friend's girl.

IMAGINE...

finding the courage to ask her out anyway.

IMAGINE...

your love for her growing steadily and undeniably, so much you want to spend the rest of your life with her.

IMAGINE...

asking her to marry you and her saying yes.

IMAGINE...

two people coming together despite religious differences, loving each other deeply, raising five kids with so little money that sometimes even a hamburger costs too much.

IMAGINE...

knowing your love for each other will be enough to sustain you and yours.

IMAGINE...

your first grandchild born with a disability so severe, he may never walk or talk.

IMAGINE...

a family rallying to help him endure his hardship with grace.

IMAGINE...

realizing that, in fact, he's the one helping you feel a greater, deeper love.

IMAGINE...

bumps in the road of 50 years of marriage, and skipping over them fueled by love.

GINE...
sixteen grandchildren later, the two of you still skiing, fishing, golfing, gardening, and entertaining Sunday dinners with friends and family.

GINE...
the two of you knowing that someday there will be only one.

GINE...
hoping it won't end here; hoping for eternal life together.

Karina is a kind and soft-spoken woman, yet her fortitude and intelligence are obviou

Make no mistake, she can and will stand up for herself when needed. Karina's photo

session took us to her high school, a place and time she tries hard to forget. Pain and

determination were apparent in her eyes, demeanor and words as she told us about

graduating at the top of her class, and doing so despite being homeless, living in the

dumpsters behind the school.

Remarkably, ten of the most prestigious colleges in the country accepted Karina, and

she graduated from a prominent university. She started her own small business, usin

KARINA SANCHEZ

courage

Kevin Sanchez

IMAGINE...

being 5 years old and navigating the city's public transportation, holding your drunken mother's hand.

IMAGINE...

at age 7, watching your grandfather being stabbed to death by your uncle right in front of you.

IMAGINE...

being 9 years old, deciding to leave your mother for a chance at a better life.

IMAGINE...

living with your sister and brother-in-law, family who are supposed to care for you but beating you instead.

IMAGINE...

your mother dying from cirrhosis of the liver on your 14th birthday.

IMAGINE...

moving in and out of homes where people yell at you, beat you, and try to molest you.

IMAGINE...

deciding to take your chances on the streets.

IMAGINE...

going to the local library after school to study, then back to school where you sleep in the dumpsters out back,
nothing but cardboard and decomposing trash to keep you warm at night.

IMAGINE...

waking up in the morning to the sounds of the janitor opening the doors, sneaking in to take a shower so no one will know.

IMAGINE...

Thanksgiving and everyone you know is with their family, being loved and cared for, while you are sitting in a cold dumpster,
alone.

IMAGINE...

being 17 and homeless, still in the top 10 of your class.

IMAGINE...

being accepted to ten of the top universities in the country.

IMAGINE...

after years of life on the streets fraught with hunger and loneliness, receiving a scholarship to the college of your choice.

IMAGINE...

walking to class on your first day of school at a private university.

IMAGINE...

graduating.

IMAGINE...

starting your own business at the age 24, helping others start theirs, positively affecting the lives of those around you.

IMAGINE...

returning to your high school to speak, and passing by the dumpsters you once called home.

IMAGINE...

making a mark on a world that didn't even know you existed.

IMAGINE...

knowing you did it all despite everything life has thrown at you.

IMAGINE...

giving birth to your first child.

IMAGINE...

knowing that your life was worth it.

BRIAN LOCKRIDGE

Brian grew up in inner city LA. After his parents divorced, he watched his mother struggle to support his family and knew his chances of "getting out" meant finding a new road for himself. He asked some family friends if he could live with them in Orange County. They agreed and he started a new life. He tried out for the local high school football team. He spent his first two years as the water boy and was finally given a chance to play in his junior year. Brian ended up with a full-ride scholarship to college at a division one school. He says his drive to change was based on one dream/intention/ thought, "I was determined to be a good father, husband and financial provider for my family someday."

Brian is a kind, generous, and likeable young man. He will shake hands with friends and strangers, always there to offer support and words of encouragement. Brian gives to others as much as he can. He mentors children and young adults, loves working with the Make-A-Wish Foundation, and you can even find him playing piano at the local hospital. Brian knows that not everyone receives equal opportunities in life; he challenges those who are facing difficult odds to take steps that will help them overcome their hardships and move their life forward.

perseverance

IMAGINE...
    a life subjected to stereotypes.

IMAGINE...
    a life steered by external circumstances.

IMAGINE...
    a simple thought that sparks a change, a promise to yourself to be a good fat|

IMAGINE...
    a thought so powerful it demands change.

IMAGINE...
    a thought so reverent it makes the world around you change.

IMAGINE...
    a thought so revealing it steers internal and external circumstances.

IMAGINE...
    a thought that soon becomes reality.

IMAGINE...
    reality slowly transforming you.

IMAGINE...
    reality breaking through what thus far seemed impossible.

IMAGINE...
    reality deriving from a simple thought to change and overcome.

IMAGINE...
    reality that sparks not only change in you but in those around you, too.

IMAGINE...
    your reality becoming theirs as they now inspire to reach upward.

BRIAN LOCKRIDGE

IMAGINE...
living a true "rags to riches" story that exceeds wealth and encompasses the true joy and love of life.

IMAGINE...
a life conquered and persevered.

BUCKY JONES

Bucky exudes warmth and love. He is a true family man. His family is so large and so close there is always someone you can call, always someone willing to help, always someone to share laughter with. Family gatherings are popular, and no matter whether it's the squirrel camp and or the sausage making party, hundreds of extended family members—infants, kids, parents and grandparents—will show up to share stories, laughter and joy.

Bucky says he outlived his brain tumor because of his family's loving support; his family says it's Bucky's positive attitude. And that makes sense, because the moment you meet Bucky, you feel as if a weight has been lifted from your shoulders, as if you've finally been able to put things in perspective, as if you've suddenly realized how much there is to be grateful for. Meeting Bucky is humbling. Despite a dire prognosis, Bucky never loses sight of what matters most—spending as much time as possible with his family.

His quiet gratefulness for every day he gets to spend with those he loves is contagious, as is his natural warmth, kindness and positive attitude.

family *Bucky*

IMAGINE...

being a part of a large family, so large there are never fewer than 80 people at a get-together.

IMAGINE...

nothing else matters to you—not fame, not fortune, nothing.

IMAGINE...

being told you have a stage-4 cancer, a tumor in your brain.

IMAGINE...

being warned that even with surgery there is little chance you will live longer than a year.

IMAGINE...

chemo and radiation, the challenges and the unknown.

IMAGINE...

that large family rallying around you.

IMAGINE...

feeling wrapped in a warm blanket of love and prayer.

IMAGINE...

four years later, still being able to see your family every day.

IMAGINE...

living, loving and being loved.

DR. BARBARA BLOK

DR. COMILLA SASSON

"It's just what we do." This is what Dr. Blok and Dr. Sasson say when they are asked about the night they were caring for the many victims of the Aurora Theater Shooting near Denver, CO, in 2012. Their humility gives you a sense of both reassurance and awe as you realize they handle emergencies every day. They thrive in the hectic environment of the ER, always able and willing to share a reassuring smile with their patients.

The six nurses and doctors in the photo represent the many medical professionals, police, firefighters, and allied health professionals who helped that terrible night when a gunman burst into a sold-out movie theater and sprayed the crowd. A lifelong bond connects them now. Deeply saddened by the many lives lost that night, they are also proud of what they accomplished. For had they not "done their jobs" and worked as hard and fast as they could, the night could have been much more devastating. Now they must focus on the fact that they were able to give some of the injured a chance to live. This community of caretakers truly does "care" for people in need.

community

Barbara Corulla

IMAGINE...

pulling the midnight shift as the attending physician in the ER of a hospital three miles away from a movie theater where hundreds of shots ring out as a gunman sprays the crowd…the flashing lights…the wailing sirens, and the screeching tires of nine police cars interrupting the silence and darkness around your hospital as officers drop off victims in such bad condition they couldn't wait for an ambulance.

IMAGINE...

the scene, ripped from a war movie, as blood-soaked victim after blood-soaked victim arrive.

IMAGINE...

the moans of pain and terror that cascaded around the hospital and community that night.

IMAGINE...

realizing your life will never be the same.

IMAGINE...

the victims—one barely four months old—with ghastly gunshot wounds to their heads, arms, legs or torsos; so many victims they are doubled or tripled up in rooms and hall spots designed for one.

IMAGINE...

being in charge of coordinating their medical care.

IMAGINE...

thinking that no amount of schooling or training could prepare you for the horror you're seeing.

IMAGINE...

hoping for a miracle to help save them all.

IMAGINE...

running on adrenaline and gut instinct, knowing that any hesitation or delay could result in death.

IMAGINE...

the team effort that night as the hospital staff—doctors, nurses, residents, physician assistants, nurses' aides, the cleaning crew and others—stepped up and did their part to ensure all victims received medical care.

IMAGINE...

nine of the 23 victims in your ER in critical condition, requiring extensive surgery, extended hospital care or long-term rehabilitation.

IMAGINE...

no deaths among the patients who arrived alive at the University of Colorado Hospital in Aurora, CO, that morning of July 20, 2012.

IMAGINE...

a night that changed everyone's life, united a community and could have been much, much worse.

IMAGINE...

a miracle.

*Written by Eric Romine, Comilla's fiancée.

NOBUKU GRAHAM

Nobuko is a humble, soft-spoken woman with a wonderful sense of humor and a kind hand, reaching out to anyone in need. Nobuko left her home in Japan at the age of 18 to go to school in the United States. She had never been here before, and spoke little English. After graduating from the University of San Jose State, Nobuko moved back to Japan, married an American, and eventually returned to the United States. She upholds her Japanese roots, celebrating commitment, work ethic, respect and humility, yet she embraces some of the more easygoing elements of American culture while making it a point to follow Japanese traditions in her community. When Nobuko graciously presents a small, meaningful gift to the host at a dinner party, she shares a bit of Asia's rich ancient traditions. Nobuko juggles her time between her family, school, and career,

heritage

Nobuko Graham

IMAGINE...

being born in a country ten times more crowded than the US: Japan, 130 million people on an island smaller than the state of California.

IMAGINE...

living in a city of 35,000,000 people: Tokyo, crowded, dense, vibrant.

IMAGINE...

a land of one race, one language, and one culture.

IMAGINE...

growing up in this homogenous place, and not fitting in.

IMAGINE...

having Russian blood in your veins and a mother who is ashamed of this.

IMAGINE...

coming to the United States at the age of 17 with two suitcases and very little English.

IMAGINE...

facing a new world without fear and recognizing how empowering such a choice can be.

IMAGINE...

the culture shock as you move from a land where society considers modesty a beautiful thing, to a land where boldness and gall is king.

IMAGINE...

feeling a rush of opportunities unlike anything you've known back home in Japan.

IMAGINE...

appreciating what you've left behind only after seeing this new and different land.

IMAGINE...

feeling torn, knowing your family, friends, and country are 5,000 miles away.

IMAGINE...

finding happiness in this new land and knowing you will never leave.

IMAGINE...

raising an American son while trying to keep him connected with his Japanese roots.

IMAGINE...

the world shrinking with new technologies that allow you to renew your connections to home.

IMAGINE...

taking all this in and feeling gratitude every day for the life you have.

NOBUKO GRAHAM

TYLER KELLOGG

Tyler smiles and exudes positive energy as he walks about the world. But it wasn't always like that. After a devastating bike accident, Tyler gradually fell into a deep depression. One day Tyler looked in the mirror, and saw someone who was failing in life. He knew it was time to reassemble the pieces and start moving again. He had hit bottom, and there was only one way to go. Up.

With no money he began a project he calls Philanthropy on a Budget. He drove through the country, living in his car, practicing random acts of kindness along the way. By helping others, complete strangers, he gradually helped himself escape his depression. It didn't matter what he did for people or how he helped them. Sometimes he would just sit and talk with a man who appeared lonely; sometimes he would help fix things that were broken. What he did wasn't important—it was about doing or giving whatever needed doing or giving. Knowing he helped gave him a profound sense of peace. The insights he gained on the road serve him well in understanding the individuals who come to him now for support, and in helping humanity possibilities

IMAGINE...

being so serious about challenging yourself that you train for an Ironman triathlon (140.6 miles) during your senior year of high school.

IMAGINE...

exercising for 14 hours and 36 minutes straight, and at the end of it all, accomplishing your goal and finishing the triathlon

IMAGINE...

speaking at your graduation ceremony about perseverance and attaining the impossible.

IMAGINE...

heading out on a training ride in college, not realizing it would be your last.

IMAGINE...

the driver of a full-size truck intentionally crossing the centerline, honking and flashing his lights at you, playing chicken.

IMAGINE...

the shock when the truck pulls a U-turn, speeds past you, hits you and sends you flying off the road.

IMAGINE...

finding yourself in a ditch trying to get back on the bike while the truck speeds away.

IMAGINE...

quitting cycling because you're afraid, but still consuming 4500-5000 calories a day.

IMAGINE...

looking at yourself in the mirror 18 months later to find you've gained over 85 pounds.

IMAGINE...

bursting into tears as you admit to the mirror all you've lost.

IMAGINE...

realizing that in losing everything, anything you gain is something.

IMAGINE...

spending months planning an epic philanthropic adventure, spanning 12 states in two months.

IMAGINE...

your mom listening to that crazy idea you just had, and telling you to "go for it."

IMAGINE...

packing your car with everything you think you might need to survive.

IMAGINE...

leaving your driveway and finding yourself on the road trip of a lifetime.

IMAGINE...

the fear of asking the first person, "Can I help you?" and the relief when he says, "Yes."

IMAGINE…

repeating this process 65 days in a row.

IMAGINE…

sleeping in a 2000 Nissan Altima during a Georgia thunderstorm.

IMAGINE…

meeting a man who had not spoken to a soul since he had lost his wife two months prior.

IMAGINE…

helping him find laughter again.

IMAGINE…

eating a can of cold veggies for dinner almost every night.

IMAGINE…

having a police officer force you to leave his town because you are "homeless."

IMAGINE…

reaching Key West, FL, and mile marker 0.

IMAGINE…

spending 18 hours alone every day, and the toll that takes on your mind.

IMAGINE…

returning home, only to overdraft by $4.02 on the last tank of gas.

IMAGINE…

walking into your house, 35 pounds lighter and light-years more confident at the end of an incredible journey.

IMAGINE…

25 of your friends reading statements to you about how your trip affected them, and how they will live differently because of it.

IMAGINE…

knowing you're in the moment where your project evolves into a mission.

IMAGINE…

being asked to keynote an assembly at your alma mater.

IMAGINE…

your local newspaper running a story about you, and things snowballing from there: TV interviews, Ted talks and speeches to audiences ranging from fifth graders to rooms full of global innovators.

IMAGINE…

pondering what comes next, while realizing anything is possible.

JEFF CARTER

Jeff was a gifted athlete in high school and college, but lost his shot at diving for

Team USA at the 1980 Olympics when President Carter cancelled US participation.

He bounced back and found his new passion: flying. Flying is a dangerous sport

and profession. Jeff's horrible accident caused a great deal of pain and suffering,

but when asked how he made it through a near-death experience and numerous

surgeries, he simply responds, "I didn't ever think there was another option but to

survive and thrive."

Jeff became a high school and college swimming and diving coach. He held the state

high school diving record for years, and coached the young man who finally beat it

25 years later. When you meet Jeff, his funny, self-confident, warm and comforting

personality makes the scars on his face disappear almost immediately. He lives with his

wife and two daughters, who support his continuous struggle with lingering medical

issues. He remains happy and never hesitates to be in public, showing his love of life

and his affection for family and friends.

survival

IMAGINE...

being a diver, full of potential—athletic scholarship offers, setting goals and working hard towards them, competing as one of the best in the world.

IMAGINE...

politics interrupting your Olympic dreams.

IMAGINE...

earning Navy Wings of Gold as an unrestricted Naval Aviator.

IMAGINE...

flying in the Persian Gulf, escorting oil tankers through a war zone.

IMAGINE...

teaching newly commissioned Navy, Marine and Coast Guard officers how to master the skills of a helicopter pilot.

IMAGINE...

putting your dream of becoming a commercial airline pilot on hold due to an industry-wide hiring freeze.

IMAGINE...

working as a helicopter pilot flying through the magnificent, beautiful Grand Canyon.

IMAGINE...

being called to help with the raging wildfires in the heat of an Arizona summer, flying over burning sage, trees and dry tinder vegetation.

IMAGINE...

an explosion, hurling you down a mountainside, tumbling across rocks and burned hillside, coming to rest in the embers, too stunned to move, calling for help but realizing no one can hear you.

IMAGINE...

57% of your body burnt, leaving less than a 10% chance of survival.

IMAGINE...

facing more than 90 reconstructive surgical operations.

IMAGINE...

people staring at you, backing away from you.

IMAGINE...

looking for and finding purpose in your life, a loving family, an adoring wife and amazing children.

IMAGINE...

seeking an enduring legacy.

LAUREN BOHN

Finding forgiveness after experiencing the Columbine High School shootings is nothing less than remarkable. Losing a best friend, and a teacher, and having the safety of your world shaken at such an impressionable age, when friends and fun are your priority, is more than anyone should ever endure. Instead of letting her world crumble, Lauren discovered her strength, fortitude, resilience and the courage to make a difference. Today, Lauren continues to speak publicly, with grace and gentleness, about forgiveness and moving forward in life. She keeps in close contact with many people from the Columbine community. She is married and the mother of a precious young daughter, Felicity Joy.

Both of Lauren's pictures were taken in front of the memorials at the entrance to Columbine High School's library. Many such memorials grace the school, all of them beautiful and heartfelt donations by an outgoing senior class of students who were present that fateful day. Columbine's camaraderie can be felt the moment you enter the building. Together, because of students such as Lauren, the Columbine community has been able to move beyond the tragedy and create "something better."

forgiveness

Lauren Rahn

IMAGINE…

waking up…going to school…eating lunch in a noisy cafeteria where everyone is talking about their weekend plans.

IMAGINE…

the silence as a teacher and the janitor run into the cafeteria yelling, "Get on the floor! Cover your heads!"

IMAGINE…

the fear as you crouch under a table covering your head, and hear a fellow student scream, "They have guns! Everybody run!"

IMAGINE…

the sudden pain as someone tramples on your hands while you crawl out from under the table, desperately trying to escape.

IMAGINE…

your heart racing as you run up a long staircase while the first gunshots ring out.

IMAGINE…

the confusion because you don't know where to run or what to do, but you know you have to make a choice, and pray you'll make the right one.

IMAGINE…

the echo of gunshots chasing you down a long hallway.

IMAGINE…

praying as you run, and feeling peace come over you.

IMAGINE…

the relief as you push open a door to the outside and take in a breath of fresh air.

IMAGINE…

the shock as you realize one of your best friends is still inside, and the horror as you learn she will not come out alive.

IMAGINE…

feeling gratitude for the teacher who warned you of danger and gave his life to save yours.

IMAGINE…

praying for the strength to forgive those two boys—who took all those lives—so this dark day won't cast a shadow over yours.

IMAGINE…

the desire to tell your story and to touch people deep in their hearts, compelling them to seek and grant forgiveness, and respect and cherish life and those within it.

IMAGINE…

the sense of triumph when you're eventually able to glean a message of hope from a day of tragedy.

AUREA McGARRY

Meeting Aurea is like falling into the arms of someone full of infinite energy and positive things to say about life. She is the creator and executive producer of *Live Your Legacy*, an inspirational TV series, for which she won an Emmy Award. She is also the founder and host of the inspirational event series *Live Your Legacy Summit*, and a sought after business coach for entrepreneurs. Aurea lives her own legacy by traveling around the country and speaking about overcoming her immense obstacles, encouraging others to overcome theirs. Her smile is contagious, her attitude inspiring—speak to her and she'll make you feel you can conquer the world. Aurea won't allow life to get in her way; instead she takes life by the horns. Her book *I Won't Survive, I'll Thrive* is testament to her determination to beat the odds, and she fulfills this prophecy every day, thriving in her work, her marriage, her family and her faith.

believe

IMAGINE…

losing your mother, who was also your best friend, to liver and lung cancer.

IMAGINE…

losing all hope.

IMAGINE…

marrying Prince Charming as a single mother of a precious ten-year-old daughter.

IMAGINE…

being diagnosed with non-Hodgkin's Lymphoma on your 38th birthday, only three years into your marriage.

IMAGINE...

waking up from cancer surgery to hear that half your lungs, the lining around your heart, your Thymus and your vocal cord nerve are gone.

IMAGINE...

hearing your doctor say: "You will never speak above a faint whisper ever again."

IMAGINE...

being cancer free ten years later, your voice loud and clear as you win an Emmy Award for your TV Talk Show and make a living as a motivational speaker!

IMAGINE...

believing in your miracle.

IMAGINE...

believing in your childhood dream.

IMAGINE...

that it comes true.

RON LYLE

Strong, fit, intimidating, and 70 years old, Ron is a world-renowned former heavyweight

boxer. And yet, it doesn't take long to realize that Ron is a kind, loving, and gentle man.

Ron grew up in an inner city, rough neighborhood. Even the support of his tight-knit,

loving and respectable family could not prevent his brush with the law, and like so

many of his peers, Ron ended up in prison. It was there he realized he needed to

change course and find a way to escape a life of crime.

Boxing became Ron's road to success, all the way to the heavyweight championships.

He did not beat his most formidable opponents, Muhammad Ali or George Foreman,

but he is considered one of the greatest fighters in boxing history. Once he retired from winning

Ron Lyle

IMAGINE...

being the fourth of 19 children.

IMAGINE...

being the only child to get into trouble, the only one to go to prison.

IMAGINE...

fighting your way through your first six months, then being stabbed 26 times with a homemade shiv.

IMAGINE...

barely surviving the attack…being declared dead twice during surgery…even your death certificate is signed.

IMAGINE...

having a vision during surgery…your mother reaching out to you as you are going down a long tunnel toward the other side, pulling you back…waking up to discover that she has traveled hundreds of miles to be by your side…her faith in you never failing.

IMAGINE...

going in and out of consciousness for days, everything hazy except a vision given to you by God…you in the boxing ring fighting for the heavyweight championship.

IMAGINE...

waking from your surgery a changed man.

IMAGINE...

thirteen years later, years of training, boxing matches, and preparation, standing in the corner of the ring getting ready to fight Mohammad Ali.

IMAGINE...

looking at the smile on his face, realizing it's the smile you saw that morning in prison, after surgery.

IMAGINE...

not winning the fight, but gaining so much more.

IMAGINE...

teaching kids—without direction, without a positive role model—what it means to believe in yourself.

IMAGINE...

many of these kids hearing your lesson, seeking and finding their way off the streets.

IMAGINE...

knowing you've made a difference in the life of a child.

IMAGINE...

knowing there is more than one way to win.

Sadly, Ron Lyle passed away on November 26, 2011.

Brendon is 29 years old. He has cerebral palsy, yet he refuses to allow his physical limitations and blindness to cloud his perceptions of life. While simple tasks that most of us take for granted are difficult for him, his outlook remains positive. He just takes things in stride and plows along, embracing the challenge. He takes each day as it comes and revels in life's little pleasures. He enjoys the present without dwelling on fear or concern for the future. His handicaps are his enablers, and he loves to interact with anyone—without fear of rejection. In fact, Brendon seems to have no fears at all. He is an accomplished musician, and can be seen with his guitar at open microphones in Rochester, NY.

BRENDON McCABE

Brendon wakes up happy every day with the single goal of making it the best day of his life, but Brendon doesn't even have to try. Walking a mile in his shoes could make us see more clearly and realize that it's life's simple pleasures that can make

happiness Brendon McCabe

IMAGINE...
waking up every day without fear of what the day will bring.

IMAGINE...
spending 15 minutes just putting on your socks.

IMAGINE...
you can't see, yet you see everything as an opportunity rather than a challenge.

IMAGINE...
spending ten minutes just to pour your cereal, and then savoring every bite.

IMAGINE...
never even considering that you are handicapped.

IMAGINE...
feeling a sense of accomplishment with any task you complete in your day.

IMAGINE...
never asking for help, but always expressing true gratitude when receiving it.

IMAGINE...
interacting with complete strangers without judgment or fear of what they might think of you.

IMAGINE...
loving music and making some yourself.

IMAGINE...
going on stage with your band and entertaining a bunch of complete strangers.

IMAGINE...
staying happy without even trying.

BILL SANDBERG

Bill grew up loving hockey, hoping to someday be a part of the Olympic Hockey Team.

His hopes were crushed after college, but he moved on. Years later, he found a new

and unique way to be involved in Olympic Hockey, one that taught him more than

he ever could have imagined.

Bill lights up when he talks about his second job, coaching the Paralympic Sled

Hockey Team. Not because he is on or near the ice, working toward an Olympic

dream, but because the boys and men on the team inspire him every day. Bill could

talk endlessly about the team players, not because the stories involve tragedy, but

because they involve hope. "The ice is where the chains come off. The players feel

freedom there. It's the trials of everyday life that challenges the players. Moving in

and out of the car, going to the grocery store, things we take for granted. They inspire

me because they don't focus on what they can't do, but on what they can do

acceptance

Bill Sandberg

IMAGINE...

getting a college job doing something you love, working with your school's hockey team and USA Hockey.

IMAGINE...

after graduation, the disappointment you feel when your dream job with the US Olympic Hockey team goes to the one other applicant with more experience.

IMAGINE...

20 years later, in 2005, getting a call from an old college roommate, saying the Paralympic Sled Team is hiring.

IMAGINE...

wondering what the Paralympic Sled Hockey team is, taking a chance, flying to Canada to work a tournament and interview for the position.

IMAGINE...

being in a room of 15 boys and men of all ages, seeing them crawl on their hands and knees or scoot on their butts to get from their wheelchairs to their 'sleds'.

IMAGINE...

the camaraderie, the strength, and the tenacity as these men hit the ice, seeded dead last.

IMAGINE...

listening to the chants, "Who-are-we?-U-S-A!", seeing the flags and hearing the screams in the crowd and amazingly—they win the tournament!

IMAGINE...

sitting on the plane home, listening to a player tell you about his construction accident years earlier, how scary and painful it was, and how he called his father to tell him he can't feel his legs.

IMAGINE...

realizing the story that is more important to this young man is what it felt like to win the Gold Medal in 2002.

IMAGINE...

deciding to take the job because you've never been a part of anything more amazing.

IMAGINE...

being on top of the world after your team has won medal after medal.

IMAGINE...

having to cut someone from the team, telling a 23-year-old, who lost his leg serving his country in Iraq, he didn't make the team.

IMAGINE...

the mixed feelings when he rides away with unbelievable character, saying he is grateful for the opportunity, the coaches taking it harder than he did.

IMAGINE...

the 2009 World Championships in the Czech Republic, your team is not expected to win, the score is tied and goes into a shoot out. After six of your best shooters have tried in vain, a 17-year-old who was never expected to score claims the winning goal!

resilience

IMAGINE ...

an afternoon in April when the sun turns to clouds and then into a blizzard.

IMAGINE ...

a detective calling you and asking you to come to the station because the car your little sister is driving is parked where it shouldn't be—in front of her ex-husband's house.

IMAGINE ...

driving through that blizzard, knowing what has happened but praying you are wrong.

IMAGINE ...

a small, windowless room, four somber detectives looking at you, hesitant to tell what you don't want to hear. There are two bodies they say, one male, and one female.

IMAGINE ...

picking up your 3- and 6-year-old nephews, then your girlfriend, and driving to your parents' house, storm still raging, not quite aware that a new life lies ahead.

IMAGINE ...

writing your little sister's obituary, planning her funeral, while tearing apart your house and putting it back together again so it's suitable for children.

IMAGINE ...

your girlfriend stepping up to the plate as she steps into the eighth year of family life in just one week.

IMAGINE ...

not knowing anything about parenting except that you seem to remember large quantities of hot chocolate being involved.

IMAGINE ...

the sense of disbelief, the uncertainty, the grief, the love, the sorrow, the empathy and the redirection as you realize that eventually you would look back on this with either regret or pride.

IMAGINE ...

waking up on a Saturday morning, barely two years later, to thick smoke in the woods outside your bedroom windows, the fire raging atop the hill only feet from your house.

IMAGINE ...

just minutes later having lost everything you own, including every reminder of your sister. Every picture, every card, every letter.

IMAGINE ...

two little boys thrilled to move into the city, excited about sidewalks and parks for skateboards and other kids to play with.

IMAGINE ...

the easiest move of your life. Nothing to box, nothing to carry, nothing to fix before you leave.

IMAGINE ...

starting fresh.

IMAGINE ...

life changing your plans, and you don't bother looking for the old set.

PAUL THORN

Paul recently returned to the area where he grew up. Family, music and art fill his beautiful log home outside Tupelo, MS, and he prioritizes his life in that simple order. Paul spends many days a year on the road, yet when he is home, his family comes first. His deep love for his wife and daughters is obvious; his smiles beam when he talks about them.

Traditional education was challenging for Paul; he was dyslexic and always struggled in school. His life had no clear direction until he was introduced to Billy Maddox. Billy recognized Paul's talent and took him under his wing. Paul and Billy began writing songs together, and still are, thirty years later. Billy is Paul's manager and Paul always acknowledges that he is where he is today because of a single man who believed in him. Paul is grateful for his life; after all, not everyone has the chance to make a good living doing something they love. He watches over his daughters carefully, making sure they get the love and support they need in whatever avenue of life they choose.

dyslexia

Paul Sham

IMAGINE...

being dyslexic.

IMAGINE...

getting bad grades in school, your teachers and parents punishing you over and over because they think you aren't trying.

IMAGINE...

feeling lost and alone.

IMAGINE...

your father being a Pentecostal minister.

IMAGINE...

your uncle being a pimp.

IMAGINE...

becoming an unskilled factory worker right out of high school, no real prospects in sight.

IMAGINE...

becoming a nationally rated boxer.

IMAGINE...

fighting and losing to Roberto Duran on national television.

IMAGINE...

meeting a mentor and friend named Billy Maddox, who patiently helps you develop your musical talent as a singer-songwriter.

IMAGINE...

starting to believe in yourself.

IMAGINE...

Miles Copeland, the famous manager for *The Police*, flying down to Mississippi to hear you sing at a pizza restaurant, later signing your record deal.

IMAGINE...

attending a rock concert for the first time in your life not as a fan, but as the opening act for *Sting* and singing your own songs in front of thirteen thousand people.

IMAGINE...

starting your own independent record company and making it work.

IMAGINE...

touring all over the country and building a fan base of thousands of people.

IMAGINE...

having a daughter who is also dyslexic, and knowing you will give her all the support she needs.

IMAGINE...

her making the honor roll.

IMAGINE...
   having another daughter who sings better than you do.

IMAGINE...
   having a wife that supports you and encourages you to follow your dream.

IMAGINE...
   not knowing where you are going but believing you are on the right path.

PAIGE BUTKUS

Until Paige was 11 years old she lived a happy, healthy life. Her parent's divorce changed everything. Her parents moved often, and Paige struggled to fit in and find friends.

Looking for acceptance, she found herself making poor choices and spiraling downward, finding solace in alcohol. She joined the army, hoping to straighten out her life, but instead found herself abused and in trouble with alcohol once again. She finally hit bottom after her discharge from the army, and realized that she needed to take care of herself. Paige now practices and teaches yoga, goes to school and is studying nutrition with intentions of getting her master's degree. The emotional wounds her abuse caused have not yet healed, but she has found ways to be happy with herself and her life.

self-respect

Paige

IMAGINE...

having a beautiful childhood and then one day having to choose which parent you want to be with.

IMAGINE...

watching alcoholism and abuse control the people you love.

IMAGINE...

being 16, innocently searching for love, an older man violently taking advantage of you in the backseat of a car, then pushing you out, half-naked, into the icy cold of the winter night.

IMAGINE...

feeling like it's your fault.

IMAGINE...

being so ashamed you just go home and take a shower, telling yourself you can wash it all away, that you can deal with it on your own.

IMAGINE...

a life of men abusing you over and over again.

IMAGINE...

feeling like a burden to your family, so you leave just to prove that you are strong, yet you have nowhere to go.

IMAGINE...

using drugs and alcohol to escape your misery, but knowing you can't because you don't love yourself.

IMAGINE...

strangers bringing you groceries at work because you look so thin.

IMAGINE...

being so desperate you contemplate using your body for money.

IMAGINE...

joining the US Army to get yourself out of the hole you've dug.

IMAGINE...

being an out-of-shape alcoholic while serving in the Army in Germany.

IMAGINE...

being sick and tired of being sick and tired, not wanting to live, but not wanting to die.

IMAGINE...

slowly realizing that it's up to you to change your life for the better.

IMAGINE...

learning about nutrition and health.

IMAGINE...

losing 35 pounds, quitting smoking and finally starting to take care of yourself.

IMAGINE...

using your experience to help others heal themselves.

THE IMAGINE PROJECT **self-respect**

JIM COTTER

Sitting with Jim is like sitting with your favorite grandfather. He exudes a kind of lived wisdom that is almost extinct. In his 82 years, he has learned time and again that life is good. He praises the benefits of growing up in a small town where everyone feels like family. "Glouster is a town that felt pride and worked hard together," he says with a smile that lights up his face. When, in 2011, his wife of 50 years died, Jim needed a new purpose in life. He saw that his hometown had lost hope, the townspeople suffering from what Jim calls an "attack of the heart". Jim decided it was time to restore what is good and wholesome about the tiny mining town that sits in the foothills of the beautiful Appalachian Mountains.

At a very 'youthful' 82 years of age, Jim began painting the outside of businesses and buildings in his town. He opened his neighbors' hearts to hope and happiness when they would first see their houses with a fresh coat of paint, proud of where they live for the first time in many years. Jim has no plans to stop his work. He believes he can clean up his town and hopes others will take note of what he has done and do the same. "It's time for folks to do it themselves rather than wait for someone else to do it for them."

purpose

James Jr Cotten

IMAGINE…

it's March 1930, and the doctor says to your mother, "Inez you're pregnant"… another depression baby on the way.

IMAGINE…

being born in the small southeast Ohio coal-mining town of Glouster, Ohio, a town with only 3000 inhabitants, but 16 bars.

IMAGINE…

November 4, 1930, just days after you were born, and two young and disgruntled miners throw down their tools and quit, their expletives echoing down the shaft and throughout the mine.

IMAGINE…

November 5, 1930, and the mine blows up, killing all 86 miners underground, but your father and your uncle, those two young and disgruntled miners, are safe at home.

IMAGINE…

having parents who love you no matter what, who make you believe that each of their four children is the apple of their eye.

IMAGINE…

growing up in a small mining town where everyone is family, everyone looks out for you and wants you to succeed.

IMAGINE…

growing up in a town so small that to play high school football, you have to play drums in the marching band, too, and perform before football games and at half time.

IMAGINE…

graduating from high school and working in Columbus for an outdoor advertising company for 75 cents per hour.

IMAGINE…

getting a call from a sign painter who needs help for a couple of weeks in Dayton, Ohio.

IMAGINE…

staying for years, growing the business, and, 36 years later, closing it down to retire.

IMAGINE…

being married to the same woman for five decades.

IMAGINE…

the loneliness and lack of purpose when your wife dies.

IMAGINE…

going back to your hometown, to where you were born, where your sister still lives, where your roots are.

IMAGINE…

the disappointment when you return to a town hit hard by the economy, people out of a job and houses falling apart everywhere.

IMAGINE…

asking the town mayor what you can do to help, and him asking you to paint the seven fire hydrants in town.

IMAGINE...

painting those fire hydrants, then a fence, then a house, then another house, and another...

IMAGINE...

people wondering why you are doing what you are doing, why you are not waiting for the government to do it.

IMAGINE...

standing at a stranger's door, a can of paint and paintbrush in your hands, hoping they will let you paint their house—for free.

IMAGINE...

buses crowded with 260 high school seniors from all over Ohio, coming to help and painting 17 houses in one day!

IMAGINE...

a woman crying when she sees her home covered in a fresh coat of paint.

IMAGINE...

cards and letters and donations coming from across the country when your story airs on national TV.

IMAGINE...

your town full of people smiling and laughing with pride.

IMAGINE...

what a little paint can do.

TROY FELDPOUCH

Troy is a soft-spoken young man who always holds the door for you, says thank you and shows kindness to strangers. Troy was born into a family full of turmoil; a father who disowned him and a mother who struggled with her own life. Finding his way in life was difficult, and Troy turned to heroin for relief and comfort.

Three years into the life of an addict, he found a way out. He sought help from professionals, looking deep inside to understand where his pain began. He fought through the physical and emotional challenges of detox. He moved, seeking a fresh start away from the temptations friends and family provided. Now Troy lives near his grandparents and extended family, surrounded by those who love and support him. Troy has been clean for over a year, he has a good job working for an equipment company, a steady girlfriend, and a tight-knit church community. He is taking college classes, and is hoping to one day repair his wounded relationships. Troy knows he must fight off his addiction for months, even years, but he believes in himself and knows that he is worth it.

freedom

[signature]

IMAGINE...

having an escape that's just a phone call away.

IMAGINE...

an indescribable pleasure, all for a measly $20.

IMAGINE...

being the life of the party, the guy everyone wants to call.

IMAGINE...

having no responsibilities, living a life based solely on impulse and the pursuit of pleasure at any cost.

IMAGINE...

your first painful day without your miracle cure, your first night sweating and writhing in bed.

IMAGINE...

waking up broke.

IMAGINE...

stealing from your loved ones to support your habit.

IMAGINE...

burning all bridges, losing the people you see everyday.

IMAGINE...

knowing the only thing that makes you feel better is what made you sick in the first place.

IMAGINE...

arms so full of collapsed veins, bruises, and tracks that you must stick yourself in the foot in hopes of finding some untainted real estate.

IMAGINE...

being followed by a specter everywhere you go, hearing her endless cries no matter how far you run.

IMAGINE...

wishing you were someone, anyone else.

IMAGINE...

trying to end it all, only to wake up in an ambulance and realize you failed at that, too.

IMAGINE...

the look on the face of your parents as they stare at the sedated wretch who was once their son.

IMAGINE...

finding hope in rehab and relapsing the moment you return home.

IMAGINE...

utter despair and hopelessness, then suddenly, a fleeting moment of clarity.

IMAGINE...

leaving your family and friends behind as you move two states away with nothing but a backpack of clothes and 70 cents in your pocket.

IMAGINE...

the first few agonizing weeks of withdrawal.

IMAGINE...

the first day you wake up without throwing up.

IMAGINE...

your first month of sobriety.

IMAGINE...

having hope.

IMAGINE...

hearing, "I'm proud of you" for the first time in years.

IMAGINE...

realizing you're not alone after all.

IMAGINE...

making amends with all those you've hurt.

IMAGINE...

their compassion and forgiveness.

IMAGINE...

finally being able to say "no."

IMAGINE...

loving and forgiving yourself for the first time.

IMAGINE...

knowing that you can overcome anything thrown your way.

IMAGINE...

being 'normal'.

IMAGINE...

feeling free of all your demons, worries, and pains.

DIANNE MARONEY

Although I don't see myself as a hero like those featured in this book, I have been asked many times about my story. I've added it to the book because it's important for me to tell others about my life. My childhood was difficult, even grueling at times, and the effects of my experiences carried over into my adult life for many years. I've worked hard to overcome these effects and sort through my emotions. And what I have learned is this: if I want to make changes in my life, I need to find whatever way works best for me and just keep putting one foot in front of the other. In fact, the common thread that runs through all the stories in this book is that it's possible to overcome whatever obstacles are in your way—and each of us is the hero of our own story.

gratitude

Dianne Maroney

IMAGINE...

being born into a family where you are not wanted, into a marriage that should not have happened; there are already two girls before you and a third baby is too much.

IMAGINE...

being left alone when you aren't even old enough to read…the loneliness, the confusion, the fear.

IMAGINE...

being 7 years old and lying in your bed listening to your drunken father hit your mother.

IMAGINE...

wondering what life is like in the homes up the street where the 'rich' people live.

IMAGINE...

your mother unable to cope with her life challenges.

IMAGINE...

being 15, coming home from 9th grade 'ditch day' seeing something unusual out of the corner of your eye in the garage, passing by as if it was nothing.

IMAGINE...

going into your house, calling a friend and thinking twice about what you saw.

IMAGINE...

running out to the garage, realizing your mom is lying in the car having done the unthinkable, the garden hose running from the car's tailpipe.

IMAGINE...

your life changed forever.

IMAGINE...

being teased at school because of what your mother has done.

IMAGINE...

feeling guilty that you might have caused her death, trying to heal a broken heart by working to get straight A's in school.

IMAGINE...

a dear friend convincing you to apply to college and the possibility of a scholarship for students with good grades who have faced tragedy in their lives.

IMAGINE...

being one of three students in your state to receive a full-ride scholarship to the in-state school of your choice.

IMAGINE...

being first in your family to go to college, later getting a Masters degree.

IMAGINE...

becoming a nurse, a job that serves you well for many years.

marrying a man who loves and challenges you, his family loving you so much you finally know what family means.

MAGINE...

3 beautiful children of your own who teach you how to love.

MAGINE...

hard work and good financial decisions, one day realizing how far you've come from your poorer days.

MAGINE...

the beautiful experience of people who share in your vision and help you achieve your dream to write a book that helps people see themselves and others differently.

MAGINE...

meeting countless people who continually inspire you, making you wonder how you could have ever doubted mankind.

MAGINE...

feeling grateful for the opportunity to create a beautiful book that shares courage, hope, love, acceptance, and peace with the world.

Epilogue

Many people tell me their heart opens wide and thoughts run free upon reading this book. Tears flow, healing begins and compassion cleanses their soul. There is something about reading another's story that makes ours a little less relevant, a little more doable. I sincerely hope that your experience reading this book will be somehow liberating for you, too.

I hope you will wonder how Karina or Doug or Marray or Sharletta found the strength to navigate the rough seas of their lives. I hope you will think about someone in your own life, someone who could relate to a story in this book. Perhaps you'll give that person a call, and rekindle an old relationship. I hope the next time you see someone—on the street, in the grocery store, driving in your car—and for some reason you find yourself frustrated or upset with them, you will stop and wonder what their story might be.

And what about your own story? If I had asked you to participate in this book, would you have declined, claiming that you don't have a story worth telling? Or would you realize that you, too, have a story as profound, enlightening, courageous and remarkable as those filling the pages of this book.

We all have a story, and I invite you to go the *www.theimagineproject.com* and tell me your story. Write it down using the word *Imagine...* at the beginning of every sentence. Start with your earliest memory and continue until your story feels complete. Cry, laugh, or get angry and annoyed—allow yourself to feel as you write. Dig deep and search for the moments that shaped your life. Find and embrace the quietly (or loudly) brilliant being that you are.

Write your *Imagines...*, and submit them to our site. Each week I will pick one story to be featured on our website. *Imagine* how your story will inspire other readers. *Imagine* how your story will impact the world and make it a kinder, gentler place.

With love and gratitude,